An o

MW00780899

EAST LONDON

Third edition

Text by
SONYA BARBER

Photography by
CHARLOTTE SCHREIBER
and DAVID POST

OUR OTHER OPINIONATED GUIDES:

London Architecture
Vegan London
London Green Spaces
Independent London
London Pubs
Sweet London
Kids' London
Escape London

INFORMATION IS DEAD.
LONG LIVE OPINION.

This is the third edition of our guide to east London containing the best places to eat, shop, drink and enjoy in Hackney and beyond – outrageously skewed to our book-loving, gallery-visiting, dog-walking, food-munching tastes. We've added 18 new places and taken out 10. East London changes daily, that's why we love it.

We want to direct you to the kind of places we'd send our friends to visit. Not because they are cool, or new, but because they are great. This is our opinion. We don't apologise.

How dare we? Because we live here, we work here and we make books about east London. And because, in a world of absolutely-everything-is-available what matters is well-informed opinion, not dry data and facts. OK … our grandfather was not born here. But nor was yours. (Apologies if he was.)

East London is now known world-over as a creative hotspot. But with that comes a slightly self-conscious hipster vibe. Do we find gentrification uncomfortable? Often. Do we like a barista's beard dipping into our oat milk flat white? Never. But do we love the ever-changing food, shops and creativity? Always. Oh, the contradiction... these are the places we love.

Ann and Martin
Founders, Hoxton Mini Press

The Regent's Canal

Victoria Park (no.39)
Opposite: The Good Egg (no.26)

A PERFECT WEEKEND

Friday night

Start your weekend with a cheese and charcuterie plate at Weino BIB (no.3), before popping across the road to catch an experimental gig at Café Oto (no.69). Finish the night with a tipple or three at Ruby's (no.73).

Saturday morning

Clear your head with a stroll around Victoria Park (no.39), then have breakfast at Pavilion (no.18) and a quick browse in Haus (no.52). Swing by Chisenhale Gallery (no.61) for an art fix, before walking along the canal to Broadway Market (no.38).

Saturday lunch

Stop for a coffee at Climpson & Sons (no.34) before navigating the food stalls and dropping in to see the latest arrivals in Artwords (no.51). Wend your way to Bistrotheque (no.21) for a leisurely late lunch and a bloody Mary, or Ombra (no.5) for a satisfying bowl of fresh pasta.

Saturday afternoon

Walk to Shoreditch for a shopping spree, stopping off at Labour and Wait (no.50), Aida (no.54) and SCP (no.55). Then refuel with a coffee at Leila's Shop (no.17).

Saturday evening

Savour a well-earned glass of something at Sager + Wilde (no.67) or The Marksman (no.65) before dinner at Morito (no.25). Head to Moth Club (no.71) afterwards for dancing until late.

Sunday brunch

Wake up with a swim at London Fields Lido (no.41) and coffee at nearby E5 Bakehouse (no.14), then stop by Mare Street Market (no.22) for brunch before wandering down to see some friendly wildlife at Hackney City Farm (no.36).

Sunday afternoon

Soak up the floral delights of Columbia Road Flower Market (no.40), stopping for a browse at A New Tribe (no.43) and Straw London (no.48), before strolling to Brick Lane. Visit the Beigel Shops (no.24) then meander down to Brick Lane Bookshop (no.53) and end up at the Whitechapel Gallery (no.58).

Sunday evening

Pop into The Spread Eagle (no.68) for a pint before catching an early screening at The Castle Cinema (no.72). Wander over to P. Franco (no.30) for small plates and wine to finish the weekend off in style.

HACKNEY: A BRIEF OVERVIEW

Shoreditch – Crowds gravitate here for the ever-expanding selection of restaurants, bars, shops, hip hotels, street-food stalls and nightlife. Fun and colourful but at times a little in-your-face.

Dalston – Centred around Kingsland High Street, this is the home of great late-night Turkish food, cheap Ridley Road Market groceries, dive bars and messy nights out.

London Fields – The eponymous green space and its surrounding streets attract dog walkers, lido swimmers, coffee lovers and a Saturday surge of Broadway Market goers.

Victoria Park – Picturesque residential streets surround this vast green space, alongside which lies a quaint cluster of local shops, cafés and pubs known as Victoria Park Village.

Hackney Central – The heart of the borough. Busy Mare Street is lined with high-street shops, council buildings and pubs.

Hackney Wick – Canalside bars, warehouses and the Olympic Stadium are found in this spacious former industrial area.

Clapton – Over the last decade this area has become another Hackney hotspot, with a constant stream of exciting new bar, café and restaurant openings.

Stoke Newington – Families, creatives and trendy brunchers flock to Stoke Newington Church Street for its shops, cafés and green spaces.

Stamford Hill – With the largest Hasidic Jewish population in Europe, this quiet neighbourhood stretches up to Tottenham and houses the Stokey overspill.

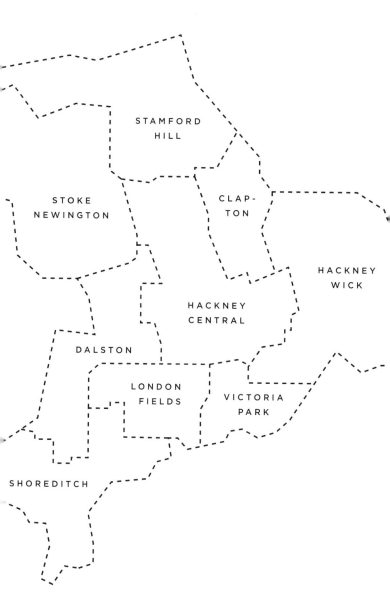

1

BUBALA

Vegetarian Middle Eastern restaurant

You can blame (i.e. thank) celebrity chef Yotam Ottolenghi for the numerous Middle Eastern restaurants that have swept through London in recent years. But this one in Spitalfields has a USP: it's 100% vegetarian, and it's upping the ante on meat-free eating. With a menu featuring confit potato 'latkes' and saffron-roasted kohlrabi, Bubala proves once and for all that there's much more to veggie Levantine cuisine than hummus and falafel. Vegans are well catered for too, though they'll have to skip the standout dish: a mouth-watering chunk of halloumi dripping in black-seed honey.

65 Commercial Street, E1 6BD
bubala.co.uk

2

BRUNSWICK EAST

Brunch café

Named after an east London-esque Melbourne neighbourhood, at this Dalston hangout you can brunch in true, supremely chilled, Antipodean style. Besides the Aussie classics – smashed avo, eggs Benny and Anzac biscuits – the well-travelled menu also features Japanese pancakes and California rolls, while the sunny courtyard setting makes you feel 10,000 miles from Kingsland Road (though there's also indoor seating for rainy days). Be sure to check out their Bakehouse too, selling takeaway coffees and gingerbread buns for walks on Hackney Downs.

Café: Unit 3D Stamford Works,
Gillett Street, N16 8JH
Bakehouse: 17 Amhurst Terrace, E8 2BT
brunswickeast.london

3

WEINO BIB

Dine-in deli and wine bar

It's all too easy to miss this delightful taproom a few steps off Dalston's Kingsland Road. Weino BIB is divided into two halves: a deli full of carefully sourced cheese, charcuterie, snacks, tinned fish, bread and ferments, and a wine bar with a few precious seats and a small kitchen turning out even smaller plates. Though it's low key, sustainability is big here: wine is mostly sold as bag-in-box (hence the name) and you can get zero-waste refills of anything from washing-up liquid to pinot noir. Just don't mix up your bottles.

39 Balls Pond Road, N1 4BW
weinobib.co.uk

4

POPHAMS BAKERY

Pastry and pasta café

Carb lovers rejoice: welcome to the temple of gluten. By day this airy bakery attracts a permanent queue with its truly exemplary pastries – chunky, fluffy pains au chocolat and almond croissants for the traditionalists and addictive bacon and maple danishes and Marmite, Schlossberger cheese and spring onion swirls for the more adventurous. Once night falls, the focus turns to similarly wonderful handmade pasta dishes: twists, folds and parcels of fresh, al dente deliciousness. The portions are just small enough that you can be bold and order everything.

197 Richmond Road, E8 3NJ and
110a Lauriston Road, E9 7HA
pophamsbakery.com

5

OMBRA

Italian restaurant

The Regent's Canal may not be quite as alluring as Venice's waterways, but you can make up for the post-industrial views with a proper Venetian feast at waterside restaurant Ombra. While narrowboats and moorhens (plus the occasional beer can) float by, this lovely spot serves up cicchetti, antipasti and, of course, Italian wines and spritzes – but it's really all about the fresh pasta, which you can also buy to cook at home. Check out Vyner Street's galleries afterwards for your own Hackney version of the Venice Biennale.

1 Vyner Street, E2 9DG
ombrabar.restaurant

6

LEROY

Wine bar and restaurant

A leading light in a new generation of restaurants transforming Shoreditch from a stag-party mecca into a hunting ground for London's most discerning foodies. Although Leroy has excellent wine credentials (its owners are sommeliers), the Michelin-starred food is the main event – classy bar snacks (like the whipped cod's roe with crisps), cheese and charcuterie, and thoughtfully crafted plates of deliciousness.

18 Phipp Street, EC2A 4NU
leroyshoreditch.com

7

TEMPLE OF SEITAN

Vegan fast food

Throughout the day, an enticing smell of fried food wafts along a queue of people waiting patiently for hangover-busting treats at Temple of Seitan's original Hackney outpost. The micro-chain now has locations across London, where they dish up all the burgers, fried chicken, fries and mac 'n' cheese that you'd expect from a takeaway joint. The only difference is that it's 100% vegan – although you'd barely notice thanks to their clever use of meat-free alternatives. It's guilt-free junk food heaven for vegans, and everyone else.

5 Morning Lane, E9 6NA
templeofseitan.co.uk

BURGER

...con, cheese, lettuce, pickles, ...o £6

SPICY BURGER

...eese, coleslaw, jalapeños, and chipotle mayo £6

HOT WINGS £5
4 wings in spicy buffalo sauce with ranch mayo (GFO)

TWIST WRAP £5
2 wings, lettuce, tomato and pepper mayo (GFO)

2 PIECE £5
2 fillet pieces with your choice of mayo

TEMPLE JR BURGER £4
2 wings with pepper mayo

MAKE IT A *Meal*
Add a regular fries + karma cola for £2

8

TOWPATH

Canal-side restaurant

There's no better feeling than getting a canal-side table at Towpath on a sunny day. Queues may be long, but are well worth it for the daily-changing menus of seasonal Italian, Middle Eastern and British sharing plates – the kind of simple but stunning food that you can only dream of pulling off in your own kitchen. The people-watching is almost as good, with dog-walkers, daytime dates and wobbly cyclists streaming past, plus the occasional swan or smug paddleboarder. Note that opening times vary according to the season, and Towpath doesn't do takeaways: this is a spot to sit down and savour.

42 De Beauvoir Crescent, N1 5SB
towpathlondon.com

9

LUCKY & JOY

Contemporary Chinese restaurant

After years of popping up in various locations across east London, this hip eatery has settled in Clapton – where it puts a Hackney twist on regional Chinese cooking. On any given visit the short but exciting menu might include pickled peanuts, smacked cucumber, Yunnan-style tofu aubergine and fried rice that's served in a pineapple, and you can even get a natural wine or Szechuan negroni to wash it down. They do deliver, but choose to eat in their buzzy restaurant and you'll find the perfectly plated dishes are a feast for the eyes, too – no surprise when you find out the chef is photographer Martin Parr's daughter.

95 Lower Clapton Road, E5 0NP
luckyandjoy.co.uk

10

FURANXO

Spanish deli and bar

Rich strips of Iberico ham and salty cheese, perfectly paired with glasses of sweet vermouth or natural wine: you wouldn't expect to find a slice of Spain around the back of Sainsbury's car park in Dalston, but here it is. This hole-in-the-wall deli and bar imports the most delicious goodies it can find from independent Spanish farmers, so you can stock up on anything from addictive Torres truffle crisps to a whole leg of ham (a thrillingly illicit purchase in vegan-obsessed Hackney). It's predominantly a deli, but pull up one of the handful of stools for the full tapas-bar experience. *Salud!*

85 Dalston Lane, E8 2NG
furanxo.com

11

THE DUKE OF RICHMOND

Pub and restaurant

Once the site of a Hackney legend – kitsch Egyptian-themed restaurant LMNT – this out-of-the-way corner spot came into its own when chef Tom Oldroyd turned it into a top-notch gastropub. Step inside its cosy but cool wood-panelled dining room for elevated British dishes like wood-fired pork chops and crab-and-chip butties, plus some memorable burgers: think roquefort cheese and confit onions. It's also one of the best Sunday roast spots in the neighbourhood, and the daily happy hour (£5 cocktails!) makes it dangerously easy to make a night of it.

316 Queensbridge Road, E8 3NH
thedukeofrichmond.com

12

LITTLE DUCK / THE PICKLERY

Fermenting kitchen and restaurant

Kimchi, kraut, kombucha – as the name suggests, this spot from the people behind Ducksoup in Soho is a haven of preserved, fermented and pickled delights. But it's much more than a room of fizzing jars. It's also a cosy all-day restaurant with a daily-changing menu quaintly scrawled on a blackboard, a vibrant selection of natural wines and 'drinking vinegars', and an open kitchen that will make you feel like you're eating at a (very talented) friend's house.

68 Dalston Lane, E8 3AH
littleduckpicklery.co.uk

13

BRAT X CLIMPSON'S ARCH

Al fresco Basque restaurant

The Michelin inspectors may have been impressed by the original Brat in Shoreditch, but don't pass up dinner at its even cooler al fresco little sister, outside a railway arch in London Fields belonging to Climpson's roastery (no. 34). What's written up on the chalkboard menu changes daily, but we can still guarantee everything on it will be worth ordering, especially the star dish of flame-grilled turbot and the signature burnt cheesecake. The freshly charred meat and fish, paired with an unusual selection of Spanish wines, makes a meal here feel like a mini holiday.

374 Helmsley Place, E8 3SB
Shoreditch restaurant: 4 Redchurch Street E1 6JL
bratrestaurant.com

14

E5 BAKEHOUSE

Bakery and coffee shop

This spot on a quiet street by London Fields makes the best sourdough in east London, hands down. Alongside those incredible fresh loaves, E5 also dishes up delicious coffee (roasted in their sister branch, Poplar Bakehouse), excellent cheese toasties and a dangerously good selection of handmade cakes. Follow the sweet, yeasty smell into their airy railway arch, grab a seat – preferably in the semi-secret garden out the back – and order a slab of buttered toast with all the homemade jams you could wish for.

Arch 396, Mentmore Terrace, E8 3PH
Other branch (Poplar Bakehouse):
2 Cotall Street, E14 6TL
e5bakehouse.com

15

ROCHELLE CANTEEN

Modern British restaurant

Hidden away in a converted bike shed in an old Victorian school, Melanie Arnold and Margot Henderson have been quietly serving up simple and satisfying British fare to those in the know since opening in 2004. Rochelle Canteen still retains its eccentricities: dinner is only served Wednesday to Saturday (though you can get lunch every day), you must be buzzed in at the school gate and you have to be off the premises by 10pm sharp, so the end of your meal can feel a tad abrupt. But the quality more than matches the quirk.

16 Playground Gardens, E2 7FA
arnoldandhenderson.com

16

E. PELLICCI

Traditional café

Opened in 1900 and still run by the same family, this Grade II-listed Art Deco greasy spoon in Bethnal Green is an East End institution, cranking out first rate fry-ups, pie and mash, Italian specials, strong builder's tea and side orders of lively banter. At breakfast and lunchtime, the wood-panelled and Formica interior heaves with regulars reading well-thumbed newspapers and gossiping with staff. Nab a table and join the buzz.

332 Bethnal Green Road, E2 0AG
epellicci.com

17

LEILA'S SHOP

Café and grocery

If Shoreditch is a village, Leila's is the local store and café. It has an honest approach to fresh, organic produce, much of which powers its seasonal menu of simple but completely mouth-watering brunches and lunches. Try the eggs with sage on a Sunday morning followed by some grocery shopping next door. Understated yet spectacular: it's a must.

15–17 Calvert Avenue, E2 7JP
leilasshop.co.uk

18

PAVILION

Lakeside café and bakeries

The one problem with this beloved café and bakery is that it's just too damn popular. But don't be put off by the queues: even at the height of summer there's plenty of space on the outdoor tables for brunching locals, families, dog walkers and morning-after Hinge dates. Stop in for an enormous pastry and a granola pot or one of the warming specials – like smoked haddock omelette or lentil dhal with fresh rotis – or swing by one of Pavilion's takeaway bakeries for a sourdough loaf and a flat white.

Lakeside café: Victoria Park, E9 7DE
Bakeries: 130 Columbia Road, E2 7RG,
18 Broadway Market, E8 4QJ and
The Truman Brewery, 12 Dray Walk, E1 6QR
pavilionbakery.com

19

SILO LONDON

Zero-waste restaurant

You might suspect that the UK's only zero-waste restaurant could have opened nowhere but east London, but Silo was actually born in climate-conscious Brighton – before moving to Hackney Wick in 2019. Ingenious chef Doug McMasters is a fiend for sustainability, and that manifests in everything from the food to the fittings: just try and stop his team telling you about how they turn yesterday's sourdough into today's jus, or about their plates made from recycled plastic bags. The worthiness is easier to swallow because it really is worthy, and the delectable six-course tasting menu goes down pretty smoothly, too.

Unit 7, Queen's Yard, E9 5EN
silolondon.com

20

BÚNBÚNBÚN

Vietnamese restaurant

There's no shortage of vibrant Vietnamese food at the bottom of Kingsland Road – in fact, there were more than ten restaurants on the 'Pho Mile' last time we counted – but BúnBúnBún is a welcome addition. They serve all the classics, but you should opt for their specialty, the Hanoi street-food favourite Bun Cha: a big satisfying bowl of rice noodles, lemongrass-marinated pork, salad and fried spring rolls. Yum.

134B Kingsland Road, E2 8DY and
511 Kingsland Road, E8 4AR
bunbunbun.co

21

BISTROTHEQUE

Modern European restaurant

A pioneer of fashionable east London eateries, after 17 years this stylish restaurant is still as popular as ever. You'll feel like you've been let in on a secret as you ascend the quiet staircase off a Bethnal Green backstreet to the airy, white-walled dining room. They make a mean pre-dinner cocktail at the Manchichi Bar, but weekend brunch is great too – especially when there's a pianist to soundtrack your French toast.

23–27 Wadeson Street, E2 9DR
bistrotheque.com

22

MARE STREET MARKET

Restaurant, bar and shops

If you want a good look at the new face of east London, there's nowhere better than this dining and shopping emporium. You'll find an independent record shop, well-stocked deli, florist and antiques dealer, as well as all-day dining, artisan coffee, sourdough pizzas and a large central bar – all under one stylish roof. By day, the long benches are a sea of MacBook-tapping freelancers, but when 6pm hits, the lights go down and the craft beer starts flowing. It could be insufferable, but it's actually rather good.

117 Mare Street, E8 4RU
marestreetmarket.com

23

THE DUSTY KNUCKLE

Bakery and café

Tucked away down an alley in Dalston, The Dusty Knuckle started as a makeshift bakery in a shipping container with a mission to engage vulnerable young people through the power of bread-making. Their bigger café space next door continues to provide valuable youth training and employment while serving up the freshest sandwiches, salads, cakes and pastries around. And now you don't even have to change out of pyjamas to devour one of their cinnamon-sugared morning buns, thanks to a snazzy converted electric milk float doing daily deliveries.

Abbot Street Car Park, E8 3DP
thedustyknuckle.com

24

BRICK LANE BEIGEL SHOPS

Bakeries

If there's one thing that divides east Londoners, it's which of the two 24-hour Brick Lane beigel shops is best. 'The yellow one' and 'the white one' are both masters of their trade, cramming freshly baked beigels with juicy salt beef and mustard or smoked salmon and cream cheese, but the queue in the white-fronted Beigel Bake is always longer, plus they have a winning edge: fresh black rye bread on Thursdays and Saturdays only.

155 Brick Lane and 159 Brick Lane, E1 6SB
bricklanebeigel.co.uk

25

MORITO

Tapas and mezze restaurant

First there was world-famous Moro in Exmouth Market, then its tiny spin-off Morito next door. Thankfully, the third incarnation came to Hackney, this time with space to fully appreciate its Spanish, North African and Mediterranean deliciousness. Sit at the grand marble horseshoe bar, order a bit of everything (especially the fried aubergine with pomegranate molasses and feta) and experience pure happiness.

195 Hackney Road, E2 8JL
moritohackneyroad.co.uk

26

THE GOOD EGG

Café and restaurant

Church Street is a bruncher's paradise, but nothing quite hits the spot like The Good Egg. Each weekend, hopefuls line up for its ingeniously innovative and creatively executed Israeli-infused food. There are eggs aplenty, true, but the menus go far beyond that with delicious collisions, such as bacon and marbled egg pita with date jam, alongside homemade pickles and house-smoked meats. Book for dinner to sidestep the crowds.

93 Stoke Newington Church Street, N16 0AS
thegoodegg.co

27

CRATE BREWERY

Bar and pizzeria

Summer nights were made to be spent at this canalside temple to craft beer – eating stone-baked pizza, watching narrowboats glide by, while sucking on a bottle of hoppy home-brewed ale. Unfortunately, almost everyone else in Hackney Wick feels the same; it can get impossibly busy on a warm evening. The good news is that its ever-changing selection of freshly brewed beers and crispy-based pizzas taste great all year round, whatever the weather.

Unit 7, Queen's Yard, E9 5EN
cratebrewery.com

28

CORNERSTONE

Modern British seafood

Hackney Wick was never a dining destination, but that changed with the arrival of Cornish chef Tom Brown's lauded seafood restaurant. The industrial-chic dining room is the place for knock-out fish-based delights: pickled oysters, potted shrimp crumpets, cheesy smoked haddock tart, mackerel pâté – even the toasted sourdough is spectacular, so it's little wonder it was awarded a Michelin star in 2021. Put your trust in Tom and splash out on the chef's selection – you won't be disappointed.

3 Prince Edward Road, E9 5LX
cornerstonehackney.com

29

UCHI

Japanese restaurant

You'd never expect to find this Japanese culinary spot hidden on a residential backstreet in Clapton. Even so, a free table at Uchi is a precious thing. Everything about this restaurant is satisfying, from the handsome crockery and careful presentation to the rotating board of specials – fingers crossed it features the black rice veg tempura roll on your visit. If noodles are more your thing, check out sister site Men on Chatsworth Road for bowls of steaming udon.

144 Clarence Road, E5 8DY
uchihackney.com

30

P. FRANCO

Wine shop, bar and restaurant

Discreetly situated under the 'Great Wall' cash-and-carry sign, over the last few years this Lower Clapton wine shop has grown into a cult foodie destination. It's owned by the folk behind Broadway Market's natural wine haven Noble Fine Liquor, so the booze is brilliant, of course. More unexpectedly, so is their food: uncomplicated, seasonal cooking conjured up on two induction hobs by a range of impressive guest chefs. Turn up, squeeze in and enjoy.

107 Lower Clapton Road, E5 0NP
pfranco.co.uk

31

SMOKING GOAT

Thai bar and restaurant

Inspired by late-night food stalls in Bangkok, Smoking Goat is an all-sensory experience: the air buzzes with chatter, chaos and cooking clatter, and although there's often a hefty wait for tables (leave your name and come back), as soon as you take your first bite, all will be forgiven. Order the chilli fish sauce wings, lardo fried rice, and as many other dishes as you can fit on your table. Prepare to sweat, shout and leave totally sated.

64 Shoreditch High Street, E1 6JJ
smokinggoatbar.com

32

THE HOXTON, SHOREDITCH

Hotel and hangout

An institution in Shoreditch since 2006, these days The Hoxton has transported the east London aesthetic around the world via spin-off hotels in Europe and the USA. The rooms are more for crashing out than hanging out, but commandeer one of the massive lobby armchairs with a negroni (and a laptop, if you must) before heading up to the rooftop Mexican restaurant to watch the sunset.

81 Great Eastern Street, EC2A 3HU
thehoxton.com

33

TOWN HALL HOTEL

Hotel and restaurant

Back when Bethnal Green council had money to burn, it splurged on a town hall in high Edwardian Baroque style. A century on, its green and white marble, lustrous teak, ornamental plasterwork and Art Deco furnishings were rescued from disrepair in its resurrection as a sumptuous luxury hotel. With suites larger and better equipped than a suburban family home, rooms that wittily blend retro and up-to-the-minute contemporary design and a two-Michelin-starred restaurant, Da Terra, you won't want to set a foot outside.

8 Patriot Square, E2 9NF
townhallhotel.com

34

CLIMPSON & SONS

Coffee shop and roastery

One of the original pioneers of the city's specialty coffee scene, Climpson has been waking up East Londoners since 2002. The competition for a coveted spot on the benches outside is fierce, and at busy times the queue for a brew and a fresh pastry (provided each day by The Dusty Knuckle, no.23) snakes down Broadway Market. On Saturdays, when the market is on, you can also pick up a quick fix at Climpson's coffee cart a hundred metres down the road near the canal.

67 Broadway Market, E8 4PH
Coffee cart: Broadway Market, E8 4QJ
Coffee bar: Old Spitalfields Market, E1 6EW
climpsonandsons.com

35

OZONE

Coffee shop and roastery

Of course this Kiwi-owned roastery makes an excellent cup of Joe: they roast their own beans and serve it impeccably via Aeropress, v60 and all the other ways the cool kids brew these days. But unlike some of their caffeine-slinging rivals, the food at Ozone is just as much of a draw. The brunch menu is so much more than your usual breakfast fare (think spicy kedgeree or corn pakoras) and both branches are well worth queuing for.

11 Leonard Street, EC2A 4AQ and
Emma Street, E2 9AP
ozonecoffee.co.uk

36

HACKNEY CITY FARM

Farm and café

East London is full of wild animals (just venture into Shoreditch on a Saturday night) but you'll find some of the better behaved varieties at Hackney City Farm. On arrival you'll be greeted by a rabble of free-range chickens and ducks, then there are the resident goats, sheep, rabbits, donkeys and gargantuan pigs to meet and greet. A strangely calming, pastoral experience in the heart of the city. Once you're animal-ed out, head in for a rustic brunch at Frizzante or pick up some supplies at the zero-waste store Get Loose Foods.

1a Goldsmiths Row, E2 8QA
hackneycityfarm.co.uk

37

TOWER HAMLETS CEMETERY PARK

Nature reserve

A walk through a disused 19th-century graveyard might not sound that appealing but a trip to Mile End's 33-acre park is always surprisingly uplifting. Among the picturesque crumbling gravestones, there's a wealth of wild flowers, plants, birds and butterflies to be discovered. Take a peaceful stroll through the woodland, or pop in for one of the guided tours, workshops or events hosted here throughout the year.

Southern Grove, E3 4PX
fothcp.org

38

BROADWAY MARKET

Weekend market

Stretching down from London Fields to Regent's Canal, Broadway Market is the place to pick up the best that east London has to offer. Fashionable, hungry and mostly hungover Londoners make the pilgrimage every Saturday to savour the street food and browse handmade goodies ranging from ceramic pots to baby clothes – Sundays meanwhile are dedicated to food and flowers. Get there early to beat the crowds, secure a seat outside a café and indulge in some serious people-watching.

Broadway Market, E8 4PH
broadwaymarket.co.uk

39

VICTORIA PARK

Park

Serving East Enders since 1845, Vicky Park is the 86-hectare emerald in east London's crown and a park for all seasons. Wrap up for an autumn stroll along the canal, take a weekend meander around the boating lake and pagoda (stopping off at the Pavilion café for breakfast [no.18], or for street food at their Sunday market), gawp at the annual Guy Fawkes extravaganza or head to one of the music festivals that take over the park's east side each summer.

Grove Road, E3 5TB
Food market: Sunday 10am–4pm

40

COLUMBIA ROAD FLOWER MARKET

Sunday flower market

Every Sunday, this sleepy Victorian street is transformed into a frenzy of fragrant flowers and foliage. Locals arrive ridiculously early to stock up on seasonal blooms, houseplants and bulbs, and banter with stallholders before the tourists descend around noon, when it becomes too busy to move. But what's the hurry? Wait until packing-up time around 3pm and you'll come away with armfuls of flowers at bargain prices.

Columbia Road, E2 7RG, Sunday 8am–3pm
columbiaroad.info

41

LONDON FIELDS LIDO

Outdoor swimming pool

There's no better place for a dip in east London than London Fields Lido. The Olympic-sized heated pool is open all year round, with sweaty, impatient queues across the park in summer and hardcore shivering swimmers dashing in during the colder months. It's always popular for pre-work swims, but those in the know dive in just before it closes at 9pm each day, when it's practically empty.

London Fields West Side, E8 3EU
better.org.uk/london-fields-lido

42

DALSTON EASTERN CURVE GARDEN

Café and garden

You could easily miss this wonderful community garden hidden opposite Dalston Junction station. A scrap of the old Eastern Curve railway line has been transformed, offering shady sitting-spots among trees and flowers, wildlife-friendly planting, and raised beds where locals can nurture herbs and vegetables. At the garden pavilion there's a bar, a pizza oven, sofas and blankets for winter, while in the summer they stay open late for drinks, acoustic gigs and lantern-lit parties.

13 Dalston Lane, E8 3DF
dalstongarden.org

43

A NEW TRIBE

Global homeware

This Hackney Road emporium houses the impeccable homeware collection of stylish founder Ella Jones. She's spent years discovering cool, independent UK artisans and old-school makers around the world – which means all you need to do is stop in, pick up a one-of-a-kind Moroccan rug, and tell all your friends you haggled for it in a souk.

273 Hackney Road, E2 8NA
anewtribe.co.uk

44

ROOMS

Eclectic homeware

Rooms owner Kentaro Poteliakhoff is the person
you want to have with you when you're rum-
maging through an antiques market for price-
less tchotchkes. His experienced eye can spot
treasure within the tat from a mile off, and he
brings all his best finds back to this magically
eccentric Clapton shop. From colourful Italian
glassware to kitsch 80s knick-knacks, every visit
turns up something different. Check out his
eccentric Hackney house on the Rooms website
(it's available to hire out for shoots) for inspi-
ration on how to piece it all together.

36 Clarence Road, E5 8HB
roomsofclapton.com

45

BURLEY FISHER BOOKS

Bookshop and café

Haggerston residents are fiercely proud of their feisty, local independent bookshop. Owners Jason Burley and Sam Fisher stock a thought-provoking selection of politics, philosophy, art and fiction titles, pamphlets and fanzines, and also host an eclectic series of book launches, readings and literary salons to bring the words to life. After browsing, head to the chilled little café at the back of the store where you can lose yourself in a new book over a coffee and a bagel.

400 Kingsland Road, E8 4AA
burleyfisherbooks.com

46

EARL OF EAST

Homeware and coffee shop

Not content with perfuming our homes, candle makers Earl of East have now opened three beautifully curated lifestyle stores: one on Shoreditch's Redchurch Street, one in King's Cross's Coal Drops Yard, and a bookshop opposite the latter. Handcrafted products made by local brands line their shelves and there's often a pop-up showcasing a particular maker. Drop in for a coffee, peruse the latest goods, and perhaps sign up for one of their crafty candle-making courses.

33 Redchurch Street, E2 7JB
earlofeast.com

47

FOLKA

Traditional handmade homeware

There's definitely no shortage of swanky homeware shops on Stoke Newington Church Street, but Folka is a little bit different. Its owner, Polish folk art expert Karolina Merska, gathers unique pieces directly from makers around Europe, as well as making wonderful multicoloured pajaki: paper-and-straw chandeliers like the ones which hang all over the shop. This is the place to pick up a hand-printed wall hanging, a carved wooden animal or a beautiful paper flower – the kind of thing you genuinely won't find anywhere else.

84 Stoke Newington Church Street, N16 0AP
folka.co

48

STRAW LONDON

Traditional homeware

Is it possible to own too many wicker baskets? The people who run this sweet store on Columbia Road think not. And it's not just straw goods here: whether you're after an earthenware plant pot, beeswax candles or armfuls of dried flowers, this cottagecore boutique sells all sorts of homewares in every natural, back-to-the-earth material imaginable. Stop off on your next trip to the Flower Market (no.40) and pick up everything you need to transform your home into a bucolic country bolthole.

126 Columbia Road, E2 7RG
strawlondon.co.uk

49

CONSERVATORY ARCHIVES

Plant shops

If Kew Gardens is just too far away, then enjoy (and buy) the meticulously chosen houseplants at these two Hackney hothouses which will fulfil all your botanical desires. Both shops are stuffed floor-to-ceiling with a luscious, immaculately presented forest of succulents and horticultural exotica with which to lavishly decorate your home or work. The Clapton branch also has an in-store café, so you can sip a latte surrounded by chunky palms, delicate hanging plants and angry-looking cacti.

493–495 Hackney Road, E2 9ED and
3–7 Lower Clapton Road, E5 0NS
conservatoryarchives.co.uk

50

LABOUR AND WAIT

Homeware

Ration-book chic is the order of the day at this unashamedly nostalgic homeware store. You'll find you never knew you needed a brass pen until it calls to you from among the speckled enamel baking trays, beeswax candles, wooden gardening tools, canvas fisherman's smocks and straw brooms. If beauty can be found even in life's most mundane objects, this place has surely found it.

85 Redchurch Street, E2 7DJ
labourandwait.co.uk

51

ARTWORDS

Bookshop

Your coffee table never needs to look underdressed again, thanks to this impressive art bookshop that offers so much more than the usual run of gorgeous tomes on contemporary art. You'll find rare imports and a hefty selection of hard-to-come-by magazines from across the world, covering topics ranging from architecture to advertising. It makes for wonderful browsing, and the staff really know their stuff.

20–22 Broadway Market, E8 4QJ
artwords.co.uk

52

HAUS

Furniture and homeware

The aesthetically-astute couple (he's a furniture designer, she's a sculptor) behind this small contemporary homeware store in Victoria Park Village have done all the hard work for you when it comes to updating your interiors. Their considered selection of furniture, homeware and lighting from both big names and independent makers is artfully displayed in the cosy corner shop, making it a pleasure to browse, and dangerously easy to make a rather pricey impulse purchase.

39 Morpeth Road, E9 7LD
hauslondon.com

53

BRICK LANE BOOKSHOP

Bookshop

This little bookshop is a love song to east London and an essential pit stop for anyone ambling up Brick Lane. Historical gems and Ordnance Survey maps share the shelves with London photography books, work by local artists, guides to East End coffee shops, hidden walks and street art (it is Brick Lane after all).

166 Brick Lane, E1 6RU
bricklanebookshop.org

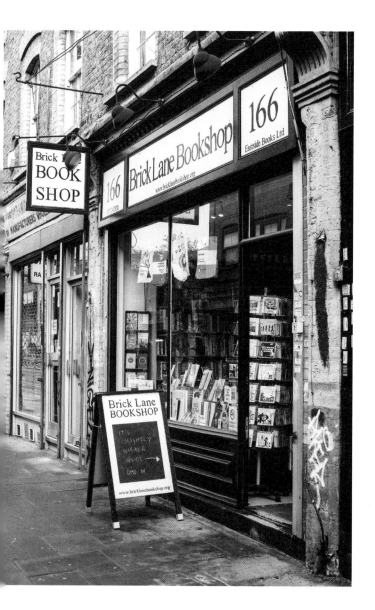

54

AIDA

Fashion and homeware

Everything at this airy post-industrial concept store has been painstakingly considered, from the idiosyncratic styling by independent European designers to the retro grooming supplies (non-ironic, honest), through to the locally sourced homeware, hand-picked book selection and vintage hairstyling parlour. There's even a tranquil little café serving cold-pressed juices and brightly coloured lattes.

133 Shoreditch High Street, E1 6JE
aidashoreditch.co.uk

55

SCP

Design, furniture and homeware

A two-floor design mecca full of intensely desirable things, Sheridan Coakley's flagship showroom has been inspiring the homes of design-hungry East Londoners since the gentrification Stone Age (1985, to be exact). Future interiors stars share space with established names, and you can book an appointment for some bespoke advice from the achingly stylish sales team, or order an array of unusual gifts and accoutrements to be delivered at a later date.

135–139 Curtain Road, EC2A 3BX
scp.co.uk

56

TURNING EARTH

Ceramics studio

It can feel like an epic journey navigating the Lee Valley industrial estates to find this pottery paradise, but once you do, you'll know why so many ceramics fans make the pilgrimage. The airy studio is full of hanging plants and potters calmly creating. Take a course to see what all the fuss is about or become a member to use the space. Be sure to pop into the nearby Lighthaus café for sustenance before making the trip home. They also have a smaller studio under the arches in Hoxton.

Top floor, 11 Argall Avenue, E10 7QE and
Railway Arches, 361–362 Whiston Road, E2 8BW
turningearth.org

57

MUSEUM OF THE HOME

Museum

Housed in a splendid 18th-century almshouse in Shoreditch, the former Geffrye Museum has a fresh name, layout and outlook. A true one-off, it's dedicated to showing the lives and interiors of the capital's abodes from 1600 onwards. Wander through recreated living rooms across the ages, then head down to the new basement galleries, where the exhibits explore the concept of home. Afterwards, if the weather allows, amble through 400 years of urban greenery in the 'Gardens Through Time', and see how centuries of Londoners have pruned their topiary.

136 Kingsland Road, E2 8EA
museumofthehome.org.uk

58

WHITECHAPEL GALLERY

Gallery

Founded in 1901, this cherished public gallery surpassed its mission to 'bring great art to the people of east London' long ago, scooping a jaw-dropping series of debut shows for some of art's biggest names – Pollock, Hockney, Rothko, Kahlo, Freud, and locals Gilbert & George among them. Leave time to forage the shelves of its bookshop (an outpost of Koenig Books) and fortify yourself at the wood-panelled Townsend restaurant.

77–82 Whitechapel High Street, E1 7QX
whitechapelgallery.org

59

TRINITY BUOY WHARF

Lighthouse and arts venue

East London is home to London's only lighthouse, part of Docklands arts hub Trinity Buoy
Wharf (where you'll also find a miniscule Michael
Faraday museum, colourful containers full of
studios and an incongruous American diner).
No longer in use, today the lighthouse houses
Longplayer, a continuous 1000-year-long piece
of music recorded using Tibetan singing bowls.
Listening to it echo around the former lamp
room while overlooking the river is a magical
experience – and just a short DLR ride away.

64 Orchard Place, E14 0JW
trinitybuoywharf.com

60

DENNIS SEVERS' HOUSE

Museum

Stepping into this atmospheric Georgian residence is like walking onto the set for a painting by an Old Master. That's exactly the effect eccentric American Severs was after, when he turned the rooms into 10 intimate scenes in the life of a fictional family of Huguenot silk-weavers, making them uncannily as if they'd only just walked out. Take a candlelit tour and be prepared to time-travel.

18 Folgate Street, E1 6BX
dennissevershouse.co.uk

61

CHISENHALE GALLERY

Gallery

In a former industrial building on Regent's Canal, this trendsetting exhibition space is the gallery to see new work by future art stars and to find out what's happening right now in the contemporary art world. Shows cross all mediums including film, painting and sculpture, and there's an exciting programme of on- and off-site events and talks, including performances in Victoria Park.

64 Chisenhale Road, E3 5QZ
chisenhale.org.uk

62

MAUREEN PALEY

Gallery

Beehive-haired art pioneer Maureen Paley moved to this Bethnal Green backstreet in 1999, making this a pioneering commercial gallery in the East End. Since then a cluster of other spaces have moved in around her, but this original still cuts above the rest for its consistently innovative unveiling of fresh talent alongside 'old' masters, including the likes of Wolfgang Tillmans and Gillian Wearing.

60 Three Colts Lane, E2 6GQ
maureenpaley.com

63

WILLIAM MORRIS GALLERY

Museum

Forget Brian Harvey from East 17; the baddest boy to come out of Walthamstow was surely renegade interior designer and craftsman, William Morris. A tour around his lavish teenage home is to be steeped in his life and work, not to mention his socialist campaigning, and will surely leave you inspired to do some major home redecoration. Leave time for tea in the café and a stroll around the adjoining Lloyd Park, where the young Morris pretended to fight dragons.

Lloyd Park, Forest Road, E17 4PP
wmgallery.org.uk

64

DIDDY'S

Bar, café and shop

If you've always wanted to have a neighbourhood bar where everyone knows your (and your dog's) name, Diddy's is the place you've been searching for. This tiny, colourful watering hole is run by refreshingly cheerful Hackney local Diddy, who will make you a mean margarita and remember exactly how you like it. Daytime is for coffee, kombucha, chats and a keenly curated 'Diddymart' – selling east London essentials like posh pasta and natural toiletries. By night, the music cranks up and the focus is on remixes of classic cocktails, natural wines and, of course, good vibes.

69 Mare Street, E8 4RG
diddys.co.uk

65

THE MARKSMAN

Pub and restaurant

The Marksman has been notching up awards since its reopening in 2015. The secret of its success is the way it marries top-drawer Michelin-lauded grub with the traditional character of your local wood-panelled boozer. Real ale aficionados, wine buffs and high-flying gastronauts mingle seamlessly, whether nestled on bar stools and leather banquettes downstairs, or chowing down in the fresh and contemporary dining room upstairs.

254 Hackney Road, E2 7SJ
marksmanpublichouse.com

66

GENESIS

Cinema

Anyone living in Whitechapel or Stepney is lucky to have the five-screen Genesis as their local independent cinema. It's the perfect place to catch new films on the big screen, showing major releases in a laid-back, arty setting as well as hosting poetry nights, gigs and festivals. You'd be hard pressed to find cheaper cinema tickets anywhere in east London. And where else can you watch a flick with snacks from the local 100-year-old bakery, Rinkoff?

93–95 Mile End Road, E1 4UJ
genesiscinema.co.uk

67

SAGER + WILDE

Wine bar

East End date night? This sleek corner bar is the place. The steamy windows and jazz soundtrack make for a relaxed, romantic setting, while staff are on hand to guide you as you delve into the small but dynamic wine list. Line your stomach with a few tasty bar snacks including the legendary jalapeño and Cheddar cheese toastie – the ideal accompaniment to… well, pretty much anything.

193 Hackney Road, E2 8JL
and Arch 250, Paradise Row, E2 9LE
sagerandwilde.com

68

THE SPREAD EAGLE

Vegan pub

Restored to its original name, this handsome 18th-century corner pub on Homerton High Street is full of surprises. Not only does it have a shrine to Prince and a secret garden, it's also London's first totally vegan pub. Not just the food, but also the drinks, décor and fittings are 100% animal-free. Perfect for a chilled mid-week burger and a tipple or a spot of dancing on Friday and Saturday nights when they have DJs until 2am.

224 Homerton High Street, E9 6AS
thespreadeaglelondon.co.uk

69

CAFÉ OTO

Music venue

You can rock up at this experimental music and arts venue night or day and there'll always be something to tickle your ears or taste buds. A great café and work spot by day, at night there's a bar and a diverse programme of concerts, festivals, book launches and film screenings. With cheap tickets on the door, it's worth dropping in even if you've never heard of the band playing (and you probably won't have).

18–22 Ashwin Street, E8 3DL
cafeoto.co.uk

70

WILTON'S
MUSIC HALL

Theatre and concert hall

After a four-year restoration project costing £4 million, the stage lights came back on in 2015 at the world's oldest surviving grand music hall. The renovations haven't plastered over the crumbly charm of this gem in a quiet Aldgate backstreet, which hosts an impressive line-up of fringe theatre, music, cabaret, workshops and tours. Get down well before doors to soak up some East End history (and a pre-show drink) in the gorgeous Georgian Mahogany Bar.

1 Graces Alley, E1 8JB
wiltons.org.uk

71

MOTH CLUB

Music venue

This revamped army serviceman's club is the perfect combination of old and new east London: a classic British institution given a hip upgrade. Many of the original furnishings remain, except now there's a gold glittery ceiling that's worth a visit alone. With an events line-up that riffs on traditional members' club entertainment – gigs, bingo, karaoke, club nights, film screenings and cabaret – there's something fun every night.

Old Trades Hall, Valette Street, E9 6NU
mothclub.co.uk

72

THE CASTLE CINEMA

Cinema

In 2016, a plucky local couple crowdfunded an impressive £57,000 to restore the derelict cinema above a posh Spar supermarket to its former glory. East Londoners can now enjoy a mix of new releases, arthouse flicks and old classics at this thriving neighbourhood picturehouse, along with a plush 1920s Hollywood-style bar for post-film analysis.

64–66 Brooksby's Walk, E9 6DA
thecastlecinema.com

73

RUBY'S

Bar

A retro cinema sign above what was once Ruby House 3 Chinese takeaway reveals a doorway to a judiciously discreet underground cocktail bar and lounge. The soft lighting, exposed brickwork and killer chilli apple martinis are perfect for cosy meet-ups. For those who want to really party, the kind people at Ruby's keep the spacious subterranean lounge open late at weekends for drinking and dancing.

76 Stoke Newington Road, N16 7XB
rubysdalston.com

INDEX

(in alphabetical order)

An Opinionated Guide to East London
Third edition, second printing
First published by Hoxton Mini Press, London 2021
Copyright © Hoxton Mini Press 2021
All photographs © Charlotte Schreiber*
All rights reserved

Compiled by Sonya Barber and Hoxton Mini Press
Written by Sonya Barber

*Except for photographs © David Post: Brunswick East; Furanxo; Haus;
Rooms; Straw London; Towpath; Weino BIB.
And additional photography: A New Tribe © Lesley Lau; Bistrotheque, Crate Brewery, E. Pellicci,
Pavilion and Rochelle Canteen © Helen Cathcart; Earl of East © Earl of East; Brat X Climpson's Arch ©
Jess Henderson; Bubala and The Good Egg (p.6) © Helen Cathcart; Café Oto © Dawid Laskowski;
Diddy's © Rachael Smith Photography Ltd; Duke of Richmond © Orlando Gili; Earl of East © Sarah
Victoria Bates; Folka © Folka; London Fields Lido © Madeleine Waller; Lucky & Joy, Pophams Bakery
and Silo London © Sam A. Harris; Maureen Paley © Maureen Paley, 2016 (image credit: Wolfgang
Tillmans, The State We're In, A.); Museum of the Home © Taran Wilkhu; Ombra © Ombra; The Castle
Cinema © Rick Pushinsky; The Hoxton, Shoreditch © The Hoxton; Victoria park (p.7) © Martin
Usborne; Whitechapel Gallery © Guy Montagu-Pollock at Arcaid, courtesy of Whitechapel Gallery.

East London: An opinionated guide (2017) was designed by Matthew Young.
Revisions for this updated version were made by Hoxton Mini Press.
Copy-edited by Harry Adès and Hoxton Mini Press.

The content and information in this guide has been compiled based
on facts available at the time of going to press. We strongly advise you to check
each location's website before visiting to avoid any disappointment.

ISBN: 978-1-914314-09-4

The right of Sonya Barber to be identified as the creator of this Work has been asserted
under the Copyright, Designs and Patents Act 1988.

Printed and bound by OZGraf, Poland

Hoxton Mini Press is an environmentally conscious publisher, committed to offsetting
our carbon footprint. The offset for this book was purchased from Stand For Trees.

For every book you buy from our website, we plant a tree:
www.hoxtonminipress.com